THIS BOOK BELONGS TO

_____

I was good to myself:

Date

Ways I handled conflicts:

Boundaries I set:

Problem areas I noticed:

I am grateful for

Reflections

BAD cut
sindy 1-21-26

I was good to myself:

Date

Ways I handled conflicts:

Boundaries I set:

Problem areas I noticed:

I am grateful for

Reflections

I was good to myself:

Date

Ways I handled conflicts:

Boundaries I set:

Problem areas I noticed:

I am grateful for

Reflections

I was good to myself:

Date

Ways I handled conflicts:

Boundaries I set:

Problem areas I noticed:

I am grateful for

Reflections

I was good to myself: Date

Ways I handled conflicts:

Boundaries I set:

Problem areas I noticed:

I am grateful for

Reflections

I was good to myself:

Date

Ways I handled conflicts:

Boundaries I set:

Problem areas I noticed:

I am grateful for

Reflections

I was good to myself:

Date

Ways I handled conflicts:

Boundaries I set:

Problem areas I noticed:

I am grateful for

Reflections

I was good to myself:

Date

Ways I handled conflicts:

Boundaries I set:

Problem areas I noticed:

I am grateful for

Reflections

I was good to myself: Date

Ways I handled conflicts:

Boundaries I set:

Problem areas I noticed:

I am grateful for

Reflections

I was good to myself:

Date

Ways I handled conflicts:

Boundaries I set:

Problem areas I noticed:

I am grateful for

Reflections

I was good to myself:

Date

Ways I handled conflicts:

Boundaries I set:

Problem areas I noticed:

I am grateful for

Reflections

I was good to myself:

Date

Ways I handled conflicts:

Boundaries I set:

Problem areas I noticed:

I am grateful for

Reflections

I was good to myself:

Date

Ways I handled conflicts:

Boundaries I set:

Problem areas I noticed:

I am grateful for

Reflections

I was good to myself:

Date

Ways I handled conflicts:

Boundaries I set:

Problem areas I noticed:

I am grateful for

Reflections

I was good to myself:

Date

Ways I handled conflicts:

Boundaries I set:

Problem areas I noticed:

I am grateful for

Reflections

I was good to myself:

Date

Ways I handled conflicts:

Boundaries I set:

Problem areas I noticed:

I am grateful for

Reflections

I was good to myself:

Date

Ways I handled conflicts:

Boundaries I set:

Problem areas I noticed:

I am grateful for

Reflections

I was good to myself:

Date

Ways I handled conflicts:

Boundaries I set:

Problem areas I noticed:

I am grateful for

Reflections

I was good to myself:

Date

Ways I handled conflicts:

Boundaries I set:

Problem areas I noticed:

I am grateful for

Reflections

I was good to myself:

Date

Ways I handled conflicts:

Boundaries I set:

Problem areas I noticed:

I am grateful for

Reflections

I was good to myself: Date

_____   _____

_____   Ways I handled conflicts:
_____
_____   _____
_____
                                     _____
Boundaries I set:
                                     _____
_____
_____   _____
_____
_____   Problem areas I noticed:
_____
                                     _____
I am grateful for
                                     _____
_____
_____   _____
_____
_____   _____
_____
_____

Reflections

_____
_____
_____

I was good to myself:

Date

Ways I handled conflicts:

Boundaries I set:

Problem areas I noticed:

I am grateful for

Reflections

I was good to myself:

Date

Ways I handled conflicts:

Boundaries I set:

Problem areas I noticed:

I am grateful for

Reflections

I was good to myself:

Date

Ways I handled conflicts:

Boundaries I set:

Problem areas I noticed:

I am grateful for

Reflections

I was good to myself:

Date

Ways I handled conflicts:

Boundaries I set:

Problem areas I noticed:

I am grateful for

Reflections

I was good to myself:

Date

Ways I handled conflicts:

Boundaries I set:

Problem areas I noticed:

I am grateful for

Reflections

I was good to myself:

Date

Ways I handled conflicts:

Boundaries I set:

Problem areas I noticed:

I am grateful for

Reflections

I was good to myself:

Date

Ways I handled conflicts:

Boundaries I set:

Problem areas I noticed:

I am grateful for

Reflections

I was good to myself:

Date

Ways I handled conflicts:

Boundaries I set:

Problem areas I noticed:

I am grateful for

Reflections

I was good to myself: Date

_____   _____

_____
                                     Ways I handled conflicts:
_____

_____   _____

_____   _____

Boundaries I set: _____

_____   _____

_____   _____

_____   Problem areas I noticed:

_____   _____

I am grateful for   _____

_____   _____

_____

_____

_____

_____

Reflections

_____

_____

_____

I was good to myself:

Date

Ways I handled conflicts:

Boundaries I set:

Problem areas I noticed:

I am grateful for

Reflections

I was good to myself:

Date

Ways I handled conflicts:

Boundaries I set:

Problem areas I noticed:

I am grateful for

Reflections

I was good to myself:

Date

Ways I handled conflicts:

Boundaries I set:

Problem areas I noticed:

I am grateful for

Reflections

I was good to myself:

Date

Ways I handled conflicts:

Boundaries I set:

Problem areas I noticed:

I am grateful for

Reflections

I was good to myself:

Date

Ways I handled conflicts:

Boundaries I set:

Problem areas I noticed:

I am grateful for

Reflections

I was good to myself:

Date

Ways I handled conflicts:

Boundaries I set:

Problem areas I noticed:

I am grateful for

Reflections

I was good to myself:　　　　　Date

Ways I handled conflicts:

Boundaries I set:

Problem areas I noticed:

I am grateful for

Reflections

I was good to myself:

Date

Ways I handled conflicts:

Boundaries I set:

Problem areas I noticed:

I am grateful for

Reflections

I was good to myself:

Date

Ways I handled conflicts:

Boundaries I set:

Problem areas I noticed:

I am grateful for

Reflections

I was good to myself:

Date

Ways I handled conflicts:

Boundaries I set:

Problem areas I noticed:

I am grateful for

Reflections

I was good to myself:

Date

Ways I handled conflicts:

Boundaries I set:

Problem areas I noticed:

I am grateful for

Reflections

I was good to myself:

Date

Ways I handled conflicts:

Boundaries I set:

Problem areas I noticed:

I am grateful for

Reflections

I was good to myself:

Date

Ways I handled conflicts:

Boundaries I set:

Problem areas I noticed:

I am grateful for

Reflections

I was good to myself:

Date

Ways I handled conflicts:

Boundaries I set:

Problem areas I noticed:

I am grateful for

Reflections

I was good to myself:

Date

Ways I handled conflicts:

Boundaries I set:

Problem areas I noticed:

I am grateful for

Reflections

I was good to myself:

Date

Ways I handled conflicts:

Boundaries I set:

Problem areas I noticed:

I am grateful for

Reflections

I was good to myself:

Date

Ways I handled conflicts:

Boundaries I set:

Problem areas I noticed:

I am grateful for

Reflections

I was good to myself:

Date

Ways I handled conflicts:

Boundaries I set:

Problem areas I noticed:

I am grateful for

Reflections

I was good to myself:

Date

Ways I handled conflicts:

Boundaries I set:

Problem areas I noticed:

I am grateful for

Reflections

I was good to myself:

Date

Ways I handled conflicts:

Boundaries I set:

Problem areas I noticed:

I am grateful for

Reflections

I was good to myself:　　　　　Date

Ways I handled conflicts:

Boundaries I set:

Problem areas I noticed:

I am grateful for

Reflections

I was good to myself:

Date

Ways I handled conflicts:

Boundaries I set:

Problem areas I noticed:

I am grateful for

Reflections

I was good to myself:

Date

Ways I handled conflicts:

Boundaries I set:

Problem areas I noticed:

I am grateful for

Reflections

I was good to myself:

Date

Ways I handled conflicts:

Boundaries I set:

Problem areas I noticed:

I am grateful for

Reflections

I was good to myself:

Date

Ways I handled conflicts:

Boundaries I set:

Problem areas I noticed:

I am grateful for

Reflections

I was good to myself:

_____
_____
_____
_____
_____

Boundaries I set:

_____
_____
_____
_____

I am grateful for

_____
_____
_____
_____

Reflections

Date

_____

Ways I handled conflicts:

_____
_____
_____
_____

Problem areas I noticed:

_____
_____

_____
_____
_____
_____

Made in the USA
Middletown, DE
02 December 2020

Made in the USA
Las Vegas, NV
15 October 2023